Travel Through
Brazil

Joe Fullman

Teacher Created Resources

Copyright © 2007 QEB Publishing

First published in the United States by
QEB Publishing, Inc.
23062 La Cadena Drive
Laguna Hills, CA 92653

This edition published by
Teacher Created Resources, Inc.
6421 Industry Way
Westminster, CA 92683

www.teachercreated.com

Library of Congress Control Number: 2007000944

ISBN 978 1 4206 8279 3

Written by Joe Fullman
Designed by Chhaya Sajwan (Q2A Media)
Editor Honor Head
Picture Researcher Sujatha Menon (Q2A Media)

Publisher Steve Evans
Creative Director Zeta Davies
Senior Editor Hannah Ray

Printed and bound in China

Picture credits

Key: t = top, b = bottom, m = middle,
l = left, r = right, FC = front cover

Carsten Reisinger/ **Shutterstock**: 4t, **Index Stock Imagery/ Photolibrary**: 4 background,
17t, **Imagestate Ltd/ Photolibrary**: 6b, Jose Miguel Hernandez Leon/ **Shutterstock**: 7t,
Workbook, Inc./ **Photolibrary**: 7b, John Pennock/ **Lonely Planet Images**: 8b, **Oxford Scientific
Films/ Photolibrary**: 9t, 12t, 12b, Celso Pupo/ **Shutterstock**: 9b, **Animals Animals / Earth
Scenes/ Photolibrary**: 15t 10m, 13b, **Jtb Photo Communications Inc/ Photolibrary**: 10b,
14, 16b, 20t, 22b, 23b, **HYPERLINK "http://www.alexrobinsonphotography.co.uk" www.
alexrobinsonphotography.co.uk**: 15t, Viviane Moos/**CORBIS**: 15b, David Katzenstein/**CORBIS**: 17b,
Ricardo Azoury/**CORBIS**: 19t, Marcos Issa/**Argosfoto**: 19b, **Robert Harding Picture Library Ltd
/ Photolibrary**: 21t, 26–27t, John Maier Jr/ **Lonely Planet Images**: 21b, 22t, **popperfoto.com**: 25t,
Photo Researchers, Inc./ **Photolibrary**: 26b, **Peter Arnold Images Inc/ Photolibrary**: 27b.

Words in **bold** can be found in the glossary on page 31.

Contents

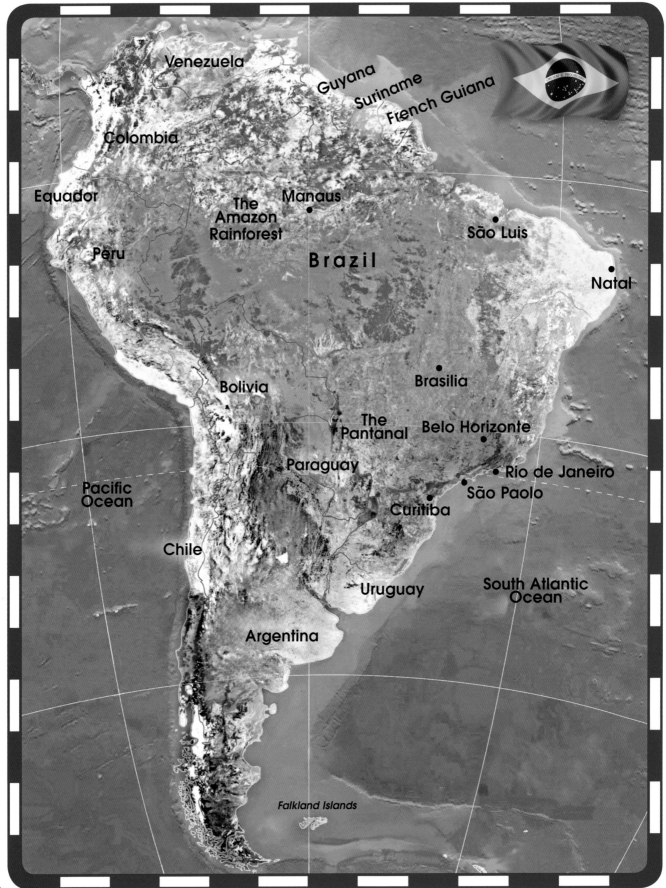

Venezuela

Guyana

Suriname

French Guiana

Colombia

Equador

Manaus

The
Amazon
Rainforest

São Luis

Peru

B r a z i l

Natal

Bolivia

Brasilia

The
Pantanal

Belo Horizonte

Paraguay

Rio de Janeiro

Pacific
Ocean

São Paolo

Curitiba

Chile

Uruguay

South Atlantic
Ocean

Argentina

Falkland Islands

Where in the world is Brazil?

Brazil lies on the **continent** of South America. It is bordered to the east by the Atlantic Ocean, and to the north, west, and south by ten other countries. Brazil is South America's largest country and is the fifth-largest country in the world. It also has the world's fifth-largest population, with more than 180 million people. Most of these people live in large cities in the southeast of the country.

Did you know?

OFFICIAL NAME: Federative Republic of Brazil

LOCATION: South America

SURROUNDING COUNTRIES: French Guiana (a province of France), Suriname, Guyana, Venezuela, Colombia, Peru, Bolivia, Paraguay, Argentina, Uruguay

SURROUNDING SEAS AND OCEANS: North Atlantic Ocean, South Atlantic Ocean

LENGTH OF COASTLINE: 4,578 mi. (7,367 km)

CAPITAL: Brasilia

AREA: 326,508 sq. mi. (8,511,918 sq. km)

POPULATION: 183,886,700

LIFE EXPECTANCY: Male: 68 Female: 76

RELIGION: Christianity (Catholicism)

LANGUAGE: Portuguese

CLIMATE: Cool in the far north, **tropical** in the north, center, and southeast, **temperate** in the south

HIGHEST MOUNTAIN: Pico da Neblina (9,823 ft./2,994 m high)

MAJOR RIVER: Amazon (4,064 mi./6,540 km long)

CURRENCY: Real (plural—reais)

What is Brazil like?

Brazil is the largest country in South America, taking up almost half of the continent. Its area is almost as big as the USA. Brazil's coastline stretches for thousands of miles and includes some of the most amazing beaches in the world. Brazil also has a large population. There are more people living in Brazil than in the 13 most populated US states put together.

Rivers, rain forest, and wildlife

Traveling around Brazil, you will see many long rivers. The longest is the mighty River Amazon, which flows through the northern half of the country. It contains more water than any other river on Earth. The Amazon flows through thick, wet **rain forest** that stretches for many thousands of miles. Over a quarter of the world's animals and plants live in the Amazon rain forest, including parrots, monkeys, and large cats called jaguars.

The Amazon River flows through the rain forest in a series of long bends known as meanders.

Who lives there?

Many different peoples have made their home in Brazil through the years. The first people to settle here **migrated** from North America several thousand years ago. They are known as **indigenous** peoples or Amerindians. In the 1500s, their land was conquered by invaders from Portugal, which is why the national language of Brazil is Portuguese. People from all over the world now live here, and more than 60% of Brazil's population is of **mixed ancestry**.

Rich and poor

Rich people and poor people in Brazil lead very different lives. The rich, who own most of the country's land, live in large, comfortable houses and often have servants. Brazil's poorest people live in **slums** known as *favelas*. Here, there is often no running water, electricity, or sewerage system.

The slums, or favelas, of Rio de Janeiro are made up of hundreds of tiny shacks.

Carnival and soccer

Brazil is known throughout the world for its carnivals, when thousands of people fill the streets to sing and dance. Many performers in costumes parade through the streets of the city of Rio de Janeiro. As well as carnivals, Brazil is famous for its soccer team, which is thought by many to be the best in the world. It has won the **FIFA World Cup** five times, more than any other country.

People dress up in colorful costumes for a carnival.

The vast forest

Brazil has the world's largest stretch of rain forest. In total, it covers over a billion hectares of land. This huge jungle provides a home to more animals and plants than any other environment on Earth—more than 1,000 species of birds, over 40,000 species of plants, and more than a million species of insects.

Jaguars are fierce predators. They hunt many types of animal, including turtles.

Some Amerindian peoples hunt by using blowpipes and darts tipped with poison.

People of the rain forest

Around 200,000 Amerindians live deep in the rain forest. Their lifestyle has not changed much in hundreds of years. They hunt animals and eat fruit and berries.

Good for everyone

Rain forests have many benefits to offer people. Rain forest plants produce huge amounts of oxygen for us to breathe and their leaves soak up **carbon dioxide**, which can cause **global warming**. Trees also help keep the jungle soil in place. If the trees weren't there, the soil would be washed away by the rains and the land would be turned into desert. Most importantly, many modern medicines are made from rain forest plants. These include rosy periwinkle, which is used in a medicine to treat **leukemia**.

Future of the rain forest

Brazil's rain forest is big, covering half the country, but it is not as big as it once was. A lot of trees have been cut down to provide timber and to clear land for farming. More will be cut down in the future. People worry that the loss of the rain forest will lead to **climate change** and the **extinction** of plant species that could have been used to make new medicines. Many **conservation groups** around the world **campaign** for the preservation of Brazil's rain forest.

Parts of the Amazon rain forest are very thick and can be difficult for people to travel through.

I live in a village deep in the forest. We get most of the food we need from the jungle, picking fruits and hunting animals. To make extra money, my father collects açai berries and Brazil nuts from the jungle and sells them at a nearby town. The people in my village are always careful not to hurt the forest, and only take the amount of food we need, so that there will always be food for tomorrow.

Tania

Farming in Brazil

About a quarter of the population in Brazil are farmers. As you travel around the country, you'll see many vast plantations. Most of the food grown is sold abroad, rather than eaten by the Brazilian people. Nearly all of the country's good farming land is owned by just a few rich landowners. People who live on small family farms often struggle to make enough money.

Brazilian ranchers sometimes use long horns to call to each other as they round up their cattle.

Brazilian farmers use tractors to work their fields.

Sugarcane

If you travel through northeast Brazil, you will pass huge fields filled with what look like giant grasses. This is sugarcane. The sugar we put in drinks or on cereal is made from this. Brazilian people also grow sugarcane to make ethanol, a fuel used to run cars. Most cars in Brazil run on a mixture of gas and ethanol. Other crops, such as coconuts and bananas, are also grown in the northeast.

Soy and cattle

In the center of the country, where areas of rain forest have been cleared, plantations of soy are grown. Soy is sold throughout the world, where it is made into cooking oil and animal feed. To the south of the Amazon, large areas of the Brazilian Highlands are used to raise herds of cattle. Brazil is a major producer of beef.

Once they have been picked, coffee beans are sieved to remove soil, twigs, and leaves.

Coffee and oranges

A large variety of different crops are grown in the southeast, including cotton, tomatoes, and **manioc**. There are also vast plantations of coffee and orange plants. Brazil is one of the world's leading producers of both coffee and oranges. In the far south of the country, there are huge vineyards where grapes for wine are grown. Most of the country's wine is produced in this area.

Index